William Loring Andrews, Press Gilliss

The Journey of the Iconophiles

Around New York in Search of the Historical and Picturesque

William Loring Andrews, Press Gilliss

The Journey of the Iconophiles
Around New York in Search of the Historical and Picturesque

ISBN/EAN: 9783744799119

Printed in Europe, USA, Canada, Australia, Japan

Cover: Foto ©Andreas Hilbeck / pixelio.de

More available books at **www.hansebooks.com**

THE JOURNEY OF THE ICONOPHILES

AROUND NEW YORK IN SEARCH OF THE HISTORICAL AND PICTURESQUE

PRINTED AT NEW YORK

IN THE YEAR OF OUR LORD, EIGHTEEN
HUNDRED AND NINETY-SEVEN . . . AND
OF THE DISCOVERY OF THE ISLAND OF
MANHATTAN BY HENDRIK HUDSON THE
TWO HUNDRED AND EIGHTY-EIGHTH

A DESCRIPTION OF THE FRONTISPIECE

THE "AMBUSCADE" PICTURE OF THE BATTERY

THE picture I have selected for a frontispiece is engraved on copper by Mr. E. D. French, after a scarce print engraved by S. Hill,* from a drawing made on the spot in 1793 by Governor John Drayton, of South Carolina, as he states in his " Tour in the Northern and Eastern States," published at Charleston in 1794.

" At the lower end of Broadway is the Battery and public parade of which I have already given you some account ; and I now present you with a sketch of it, as seen from this spot. While I was taking it the Ambuscade sailed by, having a liberty cap on the fore-top-gallant mast-head. I drew it with

---

* NOTE. The engraver of the prints in the Massachusetts Magazine.

pleasure, hoping that it would be an ornament to the piece."

To the best of my knowledge this picture is the earliest view of the Battery from the land side, and the only print that shows this point of the island except from the water, as it appeared after the removal of Fort George and before the erection of the present Castle Garden,* *i. e.*, between the years 1790 and 1810.

" L'Ambuscade," which sailed by at so opportune a moment for Governor Drayton, was the French Frigate which brought Minister Genet to America. It was afterwards stationed for a time off the port of New York, and on the 30th of July, 1793, had an encounter off Sandy Hook with the British frigate " Boston," in which the latter was disabled, but escaped capture and bore away for Halifax.

If the date of this picture were not known

---

* NOTE. First known as the S. W. Battery, afterwards named Castle Clinton.

it could be fixed approximately by the flag which floats from the staff upon the stone tower. This displays the thirteen stars arranged in a circle, the form adopted in 1777 and not altered until 1795 when it was changed to fifteen stars placed in three parallel lines. This is the flag-staff to which Diedrich Knickerbocker refers in his " History of New York" and likens to the handle to a gigantic churn.

W. L. A.

PLATES ISSUED BY THE SOCIETY OF THE ICONOPHILES

THE JOURNEY OF
THE ICONOPHILES

THE JOURNEY OF THE ICONOPHILES

AROUND NEW YORK IN SEARCH OF THE HISTORICAL AND PICTURESQUE

I T is quite evident, we think, that the worthy citizens of this Metropolis of sixty years ago gloried in the past, present and future of their city to an extent and after a fashion unknown to their descendants of to-day. This might perhaps be considered indicative of a provincial state of society, the members of which, not having enjoyed to any large extent the inestimable advantages of foreign travel (so common a means of culture in these days of "personally conducted tours" to every known spot on earth), were altogether incompetent judges of municipal greatness and grandeur.

Again, it is conceivable that the men who met on 'Change in swallow-tailed coats, and whose afternoon promenade was confined to that stretch of Broadway which extended from Chambers Street to the Battery, were not quite so intent upon money getting as succeeding generations more unreservedly devoted to the pursuit of wealth have grown to be ; and that they allowed themselves leisure for the quiet contemplation and enjoyment of the surroundings of the simpler manner of life in the primitive times in which their lot was cast when a hundred thousand of our units of value made their possessor passing rich ; all of which would conduce to a self-laudatory as well as to a calm and philosophical frame of mind. We have also to remember the fact that down to the outbreak of the Civil war, New York was in sooth a city of homes, occupied by their owners the greater part of the twelvemonth, if not all the year round, save when an epidemic of cholera, smallpox, or yellow fever drove them forth to some quiet country place necessarily near at hand on account of the limited traveling facilities that then existed. In those anti-bellum times no Newport with its princely seaside villas, no Lenox with palatial mansions crowning its breezy hill tops divided the affections and the time of " Gotham's " " best society," while now New York has its " season " as fixed and circumscribed as that of London, Paris, or any other gay capital city through which the votaries of fashion must whirl at the appointed time or not at all.

We indulge in the by no means universally accepted belief that our city in the first half of the century was decidedly more attractive architecturally than it subsequently became after it had passed into the shadow of the " *brown-stone age.*" The high-peaked, tiled roofs and gable ends, with stepping-stones to facilitate the descent of Kris Kringle with his toy-laden pack, had not all disappeared ; and the buildings that were gradually supplanting these remnants of the old Dutch regime were of the so-called Colonial order, the greatest charm of which was its simplicity and unpretentiousness. They were constructed of the best of honest red brick—set off in the better class of dwellings by marble, granite or brown-stone trimmings ; and presented to the gaze of the passer-by the Corinthian pillared doorways, graceful fanlights, and wrought iron newel posts for which as models of construction we still seek, if haply we may find them, in some now obscure quarter of the town long ago abandoned by both wealth and respectability.

Anon there came a time when, lack a day ! a stone quarry was unearthed up in the valleys of a neighboring state, and to the manufacture of wooden bowls, the concoction of apple sweetmeats, and the cultivation of Weathersfield onions, the people of that thriving commonwealth added a new and lucrative industry. Straightway an avalanche of free-stone descended upon this defenceless town and for more than half a century continued its headlong rush. When Macaulay's far-famed New

Zealander stops here on his way to visit the ruins of London Bridge, and wandering amid the debris of New York notes the profusion of this non-indigenous stone, we know not how he will account for the phenomenon except by ascribing it to a glacial moraine.

Whoever was responsible for the introduction into this city of the brown-stone of Connecticut, it certainly met with immediate and general favor and speedily became the material for the exterior front wall of a house, which no family of wealth and standing in the community could afford to be without—not because of its beauty of color or texture, but for the apparently sufficient reason that it was more costly than the durable red Philadelphia brick heretofore in vogue. The sounding phrase "high-stoop brown-stone front," became expressive of all that was choicest and most to be coveted in a "house in town." Architect and builder alike seemed intent upon demonstrating the variety of inartistic forms into which this somber-looking and perishable stone could be contorted, and the amount of meaningless ornament it would bear without chipping under exposure to the elements before the building could be sold. One wandered through weary leagues of streets (miles of which are still unchanged, except that the walls which line them display various stages of disintegration and sundry ingenious styles of patch-work) with brown-stone fronts to the right of him, brown-stone fronts to the left of him. When for relief from this dull and insipid uniformity we turned to the green fields of the adjacent country side, it was to be confronted with an equally distressing example of false taste—the suburban villa of the " Hudson River School of Architecture," in the super-ornamentation of which the scroll-saw played so prominent and indispensable a part.

Slowly during the last two decades we have been emerging from this Cimmerian architectural darkness, and have begun to appreciate

the force of what we are venturesome enough
to hold to be two fundamental and axiomatic
truths—namely, that the house simple may
still be the house beautiful, and that we cannot with impunity play with the delicately
edged tools of the Fine Arts. There is, in our
firm belief, no midway halting place between
the severely plain application and the highest
possible expression of the arts we elect to em-
ploy in the building of our homes. Cheap
art is a misnomer. It is sham art—a delusion
and a snare. Therefore, unless cost is altogether a secondary consideration, and not then
unless the designing and construction of our
dwelling can be placed under the guidance of
a master hand, the simpler we make our abid-
ing place the more heart's ease and peace of
mind will be our portion when we come to rest
under the vine and fig tree our hands have
planted.

   That New York fifty years ago was as
well paved, well sewered, well lighted, or in

many respects so desirable a city to dwell in as it is to-day, it would be absurd to claim ; but our contention that its streets offered a more attractive field for the artist then than now, is, we think, supported by the fact that when we moderns sally forth in search of the picturesque we do not seem to find it short of the portals of a building of that earlier period. Twenty years hence, when the structures now going up in our midst shall have felt the softening touch of time, New York will furnish better material for the artist's pencil. Just now it is all too new and spic and span ; but to borrow the phraseology while we twist the meaning of one of the " bon mots " of the great but erratic Whistler, " Art is creeping up " among us.

In 1831 G. M. Bourne [2] published a collection of views in New York, thirty-five in number, beautifully drawn by C. Burton and artistically engraved by Hatch & Smillie. The India paper proofs of these engravings form the most charming series of *little* pictures of New York that exist. The original drawings for these plates by Burton are in the N. Y. Historical Society, presented to that institution by the late Stephen Whitney Phœnix.

In the same year, 1831, Peabody & Co.[1] issued a series similar to the above, dedicated by permission to Philip Hone, Esq., consisting of thirty-two views engraved by Dick, Barnard, Fossette, Archer and others, after drawings by the architect Dakin. This literary and artistic venture was heartily endorsed and highly commended by the press of the day. The following criticism, which would apply with equal force and justice to Bourne's work, is taken from the " New York Evening Journal ":

" The execution of this beautiful specimen of American skill reflects the highest credit upon the *artists* by whom the views were drawn and engraved, upon the *printer*, upon the *author* of the descriptive sketches accompanying the plates, and all others concerned. It is proposed to continue the publication in numbers at brief intervals, and at a rate so low (37½ cents each number containing four plates) that the publishers cannot be adequately remunerated without an extensive sale, which we hope *for the honor of the city* they will readily obtain."

These publications of Bourne and Peabody were succeeded in 1847 by a series of thirteen plates, published by C. B. & F. B. Nichols,[6] in two parts, containing six views each, in addition to the frontispiece in Part I. It is possible that there may have been further issues of this publication, but I have not encountered them. Doubtless a continuation of the series was intended, but the venture apparently failed to receive adequate support.

A number of the views published by C. B. &. F. B. Nichols—to which half a dozen new ones were added—were used by Prall, Lewis & Co. in a book published by them in

1851, entitled, " New York : Past, Present and Future." [7] This brought about a confusing state of affairs in the print market and laid another pitfall for the unwary feet of the collector. Now, when he chances upon these engravings apart from the books to which they belong, he finds himself in a quandary as to whether they are of the true vintage of 1847 or only the adulterated article furnished by the firm of Prall, Lewis & Co.

In 1835, J. Disturnell began the publication of a series of views entitled the " Picturesque Beauties of the Hudson River and its Vicinity," from original drawings engraved on steel by distinguished artists, with descriptions by Samuel L. Knapp. Whether the voyage was originally planned to extend up the Hudson to Albany or not we do not know, but that the craft which bore these " distinguished artists " never dropped out of sight of the Palisades we *do* know, much to our regret. Two numbers only of this publication ever appeared, so far as I have been able to discover. Each number contained three full-page engravings (7 1/4 x 4 3/8 inches in size), besides the frontispiece, which appeared in part I. The subjects, all of which furnish what would be designated by the New York collector as *useful* prints, are as follows: Bay and Harbor of New York, Hoboken, Hellgate, New York from Staten Island, The Narrows, Weehawken, The Palisades (vignette-frontispiece). These prints are all well executed and most of them are very charming examples of the art of steel engraving.

Along in the '30s Disturnell published a number of little guide books under the various titles of the " Traveler's Guide," " New York as it is," " The Picturesque Tourist," and the " Pocket Annual." The plates engraved for these publications were resurrected forty years later and employed in the illustration of " New York as it is and as it was "— a work published by D. Van Nostrand in

1876. Still more recently these way-worn veterans were again drafted into service, and impressions from the plates (taken on " French India paper ") were issued in sets, comprising ten different views and perhaps more, which have not come under my notice. Still another publication of Disturnell's, interesting to New York collectors, but one which takes us a little out of our present beat, was a Panorama of the Hudson River from New York to Albany in 1846, drawn by William Wade, carefully engraved on copper and colored by hand—the good, honest, old-fashioned way of doing things.

Blunt's " Stranger's Guide," [4] 1817, furnishes six, and Goodrich's " Picture of New York," [5] 1828, seven small views in our city streets, some of which are not included in any other series.

The " New York Mirror," [1] that popular journal of the early part of this century, styled by one of its editors, perhaps half in earnest and half in jest, " The organ of the Upper Ten," which numbered among the contributors to its columns all the great literary lights of the day, supplied its patrons with a number of the best engraved and most interesting pictures of contemporary New York that are to be found. Many of them are from drawings by the well-known architect, A. J. Davis, whose death at an advanced age occurred not many years since. Hinton's History of the United States, 1830, contains a few engravings (quarto) of our prominent buildings, among them Columbia College, The Merchants' Exchange and Colman's Literary rooms at the corner of Broadway and Park Place (a building erected in 1792 by the General Society of Mechanics and Tradesmen, which, I believe, still owns this valuable property). W. H. Bartlett's "American Scenery," London, 1840, includes a few views in and around New York; and a New York illustration may be found here and there in one of those little volumes pop-

ular fifty years ago as gift books and souvenirs
—such as " The Talisman," " The Token "
and " The Keepsake"—a class of books now
coming into demand with collectors for the
examples of early American art they contain
and also as representatives of a style of book-
making (copied after the English " Annual "
of the same period) that went out of fashion
so long since that it has become an antiquated
and almost forgotten type of the art.

Among miscellaneous prints illustrating
New York fifty years or more ago, we select
the following as noteworthy on account of
their rarity and the excellence of the engraving : " Astor House, Broadway, New York,"
and " Old Methodist Church on John Street,"
drawn and engraved by A. Dick ; " Weehawken
Bluffs," engraved by Barnard, after a sketch by
Davis ; " Trinity (old) Church, New York,"
(size 11½ x 8 5⁄) drawn and engraved by J. A.
Rolph. This is the most beautiful as well as
the rarest of all the engravings of the *second*

edifice (built 1788 and taken down 1839) erected by the Trinity Church Corporation.

Those who are unfamiliar with the class of prints we have enumerated in the foregoing pages will be surprised to find upon examination how really artistic most of them are and what adepts were the men (many of them painter-engravers like Asher B. Durand) by whom these plates were executed. In point of fact the work of this coterie of artists marks the culmination of the art of line engraving in this country.

We are thus, it will be seen, well supplied with line engravings representing our street architecture as it existed between the years 1815 and 1850—the field was a limited one and is quite covered by the publications we have mentioned ;—but he who seeks for pictures of New York executed since the latter date will find comparatively few copper or steel plate engravings save those made for frontispieces or advertising purposes, and occasionally a bank note engraver's proof which contains a local view. No series as complete or artistic as those of Bourne and Peabody has made its appearance since they were issued. The art of lithography has partially filled this gap; and D. T. Valentine, who employed this process almost exclusively for the full-page illustrations in his Manual, has bequeathed us a quantity of views, both ancient and modern, in and around New York, which we are glad to have in default of better. The etcher's needle also essayed for a time the work of the graver. Neither was the wood engraver standing by with folded hands; but finally these ancient and honorable crafts one and all succumbed to the pressure exerted by the camera with its numerous progeny of processes. Now we have a surfeit of pictures penciled by the sun—good, bad and indifferent; but to whatever degree of excellence photography may attain, its limitations we claim are as defined and immutable as those of any other *mechanical* art. That the most highly perfected photographic process yet invented is capable of producing a work of art in the high sense of the term, we are not willing to admit; nor will it be until some ray has been discovered more weird and potent than that of Röntgen, which can transmit to the sensitized plate in its dark recess the creative mental faculty itself as well as the image of the thing created. Until that day dawns the camera will continue to perform its appointed tasks like the obedient but senseless automaton that it is, and nothing more.

It was in emulation of and to supplement, as far as might be, these publications of Bourne and Peabody that the Society of Iconophiles was founded in 1895 and set itself to the pleasant task of picturing New York as it is in the closing years of the century, while incidentally it hoped to revive an interest in and to encourage the practice of the long neglected art of pure line engraving.

The Society has issued, up to the present time, twelve plates of subjects selected for their historical and, as far as possible, pictorial value. It began with time-honored St. Paul's, the oldest of our ecclesiastical edifices (opened for divine worship on the 30th of October, 1766). The many earlier views of this building, beginning with the first and rarest—the one published in the New York Magazine in 1795—have been taken, almost without exception, from the Broadway side. This of the Iconophiles is a view from Vesey street and shows the front of the chapel (facing the North river) and a portion of the graveyard where, undisturbed by the countless throngs that daily hurry past the enclosure, St. Paul's old parishioners sleep on, under the "easie earth that covers them." It is a winter's landscape and the leafless branches of the trees permitted our artist to depict the architectural details of the fine old structure and the graceful spire which we have lived to see far overtopped by a building devoted to secular uses. St. Paul's was designed by a Mr. McBean, a Scotchman, who is said to have been a pupil of James Gibbs, the architect of the London Church of St. Martins-in-the-Fields, which took the place of the structure of the same name wherein Archbishop Tenison once preached a " notable sermon in praise of Ellen Gwyn." St. Paul's resembles in some of its exterior and interior features St. Martins-in-the-Fields, which is considered one of the finest of the London churches of its age and class.

Publication No. 2 opens the doors of this ancient and venerable edifice and affords a view of the chancel with the pulpit standing on the north side of the choir to which it had been removed in 1879, as noted in the short description of the plates, printed on the wrapper which accompanies each issue of the Society. Other changes that have taken place from time to time in the interior of St. Paul's are noted by Dr. Morgan Dix in his " Historical

Recollections of the Chapel," who also recounts the number of times that the building has been threatened with destruction by fire. First in 1776 in the *great* fire, which consumed about one-eighth of the city, including Trinity Church. Second, in 1799, by a fire in Vesey street, during which the steeple of St. Paul's was in flames. Third and fourth, in 1820 and 1848, when for the first and second times Park Theatre, in Park Row, was burnt; and fifth, in 1865 at the burning of Barnum's American Museum, which then occupied the present site of the new twenty-five storied St. Paul Building (307 feet high) on the corner of Broadway and Ann street. With so many towering fire-proof structures in the neighborhood to protect it, the custodians of St. Paul's should sleep more quietly o'nights, and enjoy a feeling of security from attacks of the fire fiend which heretofore they have not known. Publication No. 3 is a view of Fraunces's Tavern on the south-east corner of Broad and

Pearl streets. So much has been said and written of late years concerning this building and it has been brought into such prominence by " Sons of the Revolution " and other patriotic bodies, that the very gamins of the street should be familiar with the succession of historical events that have made the tavern, kept by Samuel Fraunces, ex-steward in the household of President Washington, famous for all time.

Publication No. 4.—For the subject of this plate the artist to the Society, Mr. E. Davis French, traversed nearly the entire length of the island until he entered the gateway to the Roger Morris House. This relict of pre-revolutionary times is described as follows in the brief account prefixed to the plate :

" The Roger Morris House, Washington Heights, near 161st Street." " Built about the middle of the last century by Colonel Roger Morris, aide-de-camp to General Braddock in the expedition against Fort Duquesne."

In 1776 it was the headquarters of General Washington, and after the capture of the island by the British was occupied by the Hessian General Kniphausen. In 1779 the property was sold under the act of attainder, passed that year by the legislature of the State of New York, and passed out of the possession of the family. After several changes of ownership the house became the property of Stephen Jumel, a French wine merchant engaged in business in New York, by whom it was devised to his widow, who afterward became the wife of Aaron Burr. It is now the residence of General Ferdinand P. Earle.

Publication No. 5.—The material for the next issue of the Society was found in the neighborhood of the Roger Morris House. Hamilton Grange, depicted in this plate, was built by Alexander Hamilton about 1802. Only two years later, July 11, 1804, New York was startled by the appearance of a bulletin announcing that General Hamilton was shot that morning in a duel by Colonel Burr, and was said to be mortally wounded. His death occurred the next afternoon at 2 o'clock. The " Grange " remained in possession of the family until 1845. It has lately been moved a couple of blocks away from its original site, and now stands at the corner of 141st street and Convent avenue. It is at present occupied as the Rectory of St. Luke's Protestant Episcopal Church.

Publication No. 6 compels us to retrace our steps and turn our faces eastward to St. Mark's Church in the Bowery (Second ave. 10th and 11th streets). Next to St. Paul's this is the oldest church edifice in the city. It was built during the years 1795–1799, on ground which formed a part of the " bouwery " or farm purchased by Governor Stuyvesant in 1651 for 6,400 guilders, or £1,066, and was donated to the Episcopal Church in 1793 by his great grandson, Petrus Stuyvesant. The following is copied from Dr. Anthon's Parish Annals of St. Mark's Church:

"Governor Stuyvesant arrived in this country in 1647. He soon afterwards purchased a farm which became distinctively known as the 'Bouwery' (the Dutch word for farm). The Bowery, the name of one of the principal streets in our city, is derived from it. For the accommodation of his family and the few residents in the neighborhood, the Governor, at his own expense, erected an edifice for worship (according to the rites of the Dutch Reformed Church) on his farm, on the very site where St. Mark's Church now stands."

Publication No. 7 is a View of the City Hall in the Park. Because of its importance as a municipal building as well as on account of its satisfactory character as a piece of architecture, more pictures have been made of the City Hall than of any other of our public edifices. Nevertheless, the Iconophiles decided to include it in their series, doubtless upon the ground that a collection of "Views in New York" without the City Hall would resemble too much the play of Hamlet with Hamlet left out. Every good citizen is presumed to know that the corner stone of the City Hall was laid May 26th, 1803, and that it was finished in 1812, at a cost of half a million dollars. In the past ten or twelve years this building has been repeatedly threatened with demolition by our sage and æsthetic city fathers; but public opinion has thus far proved sufficiently potent to avert this fate, and the building has not changed in outward appearance since in the year 1819 Fitz-Greene Halleck entertained his fellow townsmen with this poetical description of the statue which then as now surmounted the dome of the City Hall:

" *And on our City Hall a Justice stands—*
   A neater form was never made of board—
Holding majestically in her hands
   A pair of steelyards and a wooden sword,
And looking down with complacent civility
Emblem of dignity and durability."

Publication No. 8 is a " Prospect " of that gloomy pile of buildings, seldom if ever referred to by its proper name, " The Halls of Justice," but known in common parlance as " The Tombs"—an appropriate title, as it indicates its architectural origin, " An Egyptian tomb," as well as the melancholy uses for which it was constructed—upon made ground in about the center of what was once the old Collect pond.   It came to the ears of the Iconophiles that the removal of this building was in contemplation ; and so they hastened to make a pictorial note of a structure which is of more profound interest to certain classes in this community than any other building belonging to the Municipality, of which unhappily they constitute neither useful nor ornamental members.

Publication No. 9 is a picture of the National Academy of Design.   This building, copied after the Doges' Palace in Venice, has stood in the midst of its incongruous surroundings on the northwest corner of Twenty-third street and Fourth avenue for more than thirty years, with the prosaic tinkle of street-car bells echoing through its vaulted arches in lieu of the musical cry of the gay gondolier. It is an unfinished edifice, as the decoration of the exterior has never been completed, nor ever will be, as the days of this example of the " revived gothic order " of architecture are numbered, and the building will shortly be razed to the ground by its new proprietors, the Metropolitan Life Insurance Company of New York.

Publication No. 10 presents a view of St. John's Chapel. This building was erected during the years 1803 to 1807 at a cost of about $200,000. It stands on the east side of Varick street, between Beach and Laight, and at the time of its erection fronted a park known as Hudson Square, later as St. John's Park,[8] a pleasant enclosure shaded with fine old trees—the ground having at one time formed

part of the Anneke Jans Bogardus estate.
This park was sold early in 1869 to the Hudson River Railroad Company, and a freight
station took the place of one of the breathing
spots with which lower New York was then,
as it is still, all too scantily supplied—a public need that we have recognized and attempted
to supply only within the past few years.   It
is a satisfaction to feel that the more enlightened sense of this community would not now
regard with equanimity the blotting out of a
pleasure ground like this from the map of
New York City.   Let us hope that the time
may come when public opinion will demand
the restoration of St. John's Park, and that
once again through the doorways of the old
church will float the sound of rustling leaves
and the twittering of birds instead of the roar
of wheels and the noise of escaping steam.
Meanwhile the people of the neighborhood
should enter a protest against the unnecessarily unseemly appearance of the walls of this

huge, ungainly structure, covered with post bills of every description from end to end.

Publication No. 11 is a view of the Fifth avenue front of the Murray Hill Distributing Reservoir. The capacity of this reservoir, which now plays so insignificant a part in the city's system of water works, is 20,000,000 gallons. As an interesting bit of ancient history in this connection we may recall the proposal made by Christopher Colles immediately prior to the Revolutionary war to build a reservoir on open ground near the new jail (Pearl and White streets), with a capacity of 1,200,-000 gallons, for furnishing the City of New York with a constant supply of fresh water. Mr. Colles enters into the following calculation, "shewing the utility of his design," which we quote because it helps us to realize how little more than a good-sized village our city was so late as 1774:

"It is supposed that there are 3,000 Houses that receive Water from the Tea

Water Men ; that at the least, upon an Average, each House pays One Penny Half-penny per day for this Water ; this makes the Sum of £6,750 per Annum, which is 45s for each Houfe per Annum. According to the Design proposed, there will be paid £6,000 per annum for four Years, which is 40s each House : By which it appears that even while the Works are paying for, there will be a saving made to the City of £750 per annum, and after the said four Yeares, as the Tax will not be more than 10s per annum to be paid by each houfe, it is evident that there will be saved to the city, the yearly sum of £5,250 *for ever."* The Revolutionary War interfered with the consideration of this project.

Wm. L. Stone, in his History of New York City, published in 1872, supplies a description of the Murray Hill Reservoir, an abstract from which will spare us the necessity of making a new survey, and answer our present purpose quite as well if not better.

" Its walls are of dark granite and average 44 feet in height above the adjacent streets. Upon the top of the wall, which is reached by massive steps, is a broad promenade from which may be obtained a fine view of the surrounding country. Perfect security for the visitor is obtained by a strong battlement of granite (and an iron railing) on the outside, and an iron fence on the inside nearest the water. The water was first let into this building on the 4th of July, 1842 (Mr. Haswell says the 5th), and on the 14th of the following October distributed by means of iron pipes throughout the city."

The public celebration, which was held upon this occasion, rivaled in its pageantry the great "jubilee," which upon the completion of the Erie Canal in 1825 (October 26th) " married this city to the mighty west," or the grand procession which, in 1788, celebrated the adoption of the Federal Constitution.

The view from the promenade is not now so extensive as above described, by reason of the tall buildings erected in the neighborhood in recent years, and a luxuriant growth of the ampelopsis vine hides and beautifies during the greater part of the year most of the somber granite walls of the structure. The building will probably ere long be removed, and the ground become the site (unexcelled in New York for such a purpose) of the New York Public Library — that combination lately effected between the Astor, Lenox and Tilden foundations, the formation of which is so characteristic of the tendency toward concentration of effort which is the drift of the times.

Publication No. 12 and last, " The Bowling Green."—This small circular park, originally used as a ball and quoit ground by the good folk of New Amsterdam, was laid out in 1733, when by a city ordinance it was " Resolved that the Corporation lease a piece of ground lying at the lower end of Broadway fronting the Fort, under the annual rent of a peppercorn."

On May 17th, 1770, an equestrian statue

of George III. was ordered to be erected in the " Bowling Green." This statue was cut off in the very flower of its youth. On July 8th, 1776, amid shouts and the ringing of liberty bells, it was destroyed by the populace, and the lead of which it was composed cast into bullets. This is a thrice-told tale and, like a number which are narrated in connection with Fraunces's Tavern, is rather withered by age and battered by repetition. These stock stories of old New York are standard goods, kept constantly on hand and must be expected to become occasionally a little stale and shop-worn. The only statue that has been admitted within this enclosure since the summary ejectment of the leaden effigy of King George is one of Abraham de Peyster, recently erected in the southwest corner of the little park.

The block of seven houses seen in the picture fronting the Bowling Green, was erected upon the site of the old Fort and

Government House,[9] which latter building was removed in 1815. For many years these houses ranked among the finest and most fashionable private residences in the city; but they have long been given over to business purposes. They are at present occupied mostly by the offices of various Transatlantic steamship companies, and of foreign consulates. On the right of the picture we have a glimpse of the Battery and the waters of the Bay.

Here at the southernmost point of the island the Iconophiles break their journey. The Society has decreed that the twelve plates now issued shall constitute a series. The first stage of its antiquarian and sentimental journey therefore is completed, so we close the leaves of our sketch-book and wend our way homewards over the " Battery walk," that " pleasant promenade," still the " ornament and the pride of the island of Manna-hatta " as it has ever been since the day when the corpulent

Dutch burgher first peacefully puffed his long-stemmed pipe in the afternoon shade of its drooping willows and wide-spreading sycamores, and through the encircling wreaths of smoke gazed dreamily upon the "noblest prospect in the whole known world."

Envoy.

In parting company for a time at least with the fifty subscribers to our illustrated itinerary, we trust that these fellow tourists of ours have found the pilgrimage an instructive one, are not travel-stained and weary, and have enjoyed equally with their guides, the Iconophiles, this ramble around the streets of our fair City of New York.

WILLIAM LORING ANDREWS.

NOTES AND LISTS
OF NEW YORK VIEWS

NOTES AND LISTS
OF NEW YORK VIEWS

NOTE I

THE "New York Mirror" was founded in 1824 by Saml. Woodworth, the author of the "Old Oaken Bucket," and continued by Geo. P. Morris, N. P. Willis and Theo. S. Fay. Many of the fine engravings in this Journal were the work of Asher B. Durand and James Smillie. The FULL page illustrations average about 9 x 6 inches in size. The prints marked "S" are vignettes, six on a sheet, eighteen in all.

VIEWS IN AND ABOUT NEW YORK

Jews' Synagogue, Elm Street (S) . " vii., 1829
Lafayette Theater . . . . " v., 1828
Lunatic Asylum, Bloomingdale . . . " xi., 1834
Merchants' Exchange (S) . . . . " vii., 1829
Masonic Hall (S) . . . . . " vii., 1829
Middle Dutch Church, Nassau Street . . " vii., 1829
New York from Brooklyn Heights . . " xi., 1834
New York from Bedloe's Island . . " xiv., 1837
New York from Jersey City . . . . " viii., 1831
New York Institution for the Instruction of the
    Deaf and Dumb . . . . . " xiii., 1835
North Battery, foot of Hubert Street . . . " xi., 1833
North Dutch Church, William Street (S) . . " vii., 1829
Old Times on Broadway . . . . . " xiv., 1836
Palisades (The) View on the Hudson . . . " xvi., 1838
Park Row . . . . " viii., 1830
Presbyterian Church, Cedar Street (S) . . . " vii., 1829
Reformed Presbyterian Church, Murray Street (S) . " vii., 1829
Rotunda (The), Chamber Street (S) . . . " vii., 1829
South Dutch Church, Exchange Place (S) . . " vii., 1829
St. George's Church (S) . . . . . " vii., 1829
St. John's Chapel . . . . . . " vi., 1829
St. Mark's Church (S) . . . . . " vii., 1829
St. Paul's Chapel . . . . . . " v., 1828
St. Patrick's Cathedral (S) . . . . " vii., 1829
St. Thomas's Church . . . . . " vi., 1829
Trinity Church . . . . . . " v., 1828
U. S. Branch Bank (S) . . . . . " vii., 1829
Unitarian Church, Mercer Street (S) . . " vii., 1829
Wall Street . . . . " ix., 1832
Weehawken . . . . " x., 1833
Wood Scene near Hoboken . . . . " x., 1832

In addition to the views above enumerated the
"New York Mirror" contains finely engraved por-

traits of the following literary and dramatic celebrities of the day: James H. Hackett, N. P. Willis, Fitz-Greene Halleck, Washington Irving, William Cullen Bryant, Charles S. Sprague, Miss C. M. Sedgewick and Prosper M. Wetmore.

NOTE II

Titles of plates in " BOURNE'S VIEWS," quarto. Size of print 3½x2¾ (two on a page), all but " New York from Weehawk," which is 5¾x3¾.

American Hotel, Broadway
Bay and Harbor of New York
Bowery Theater
Bowling Green, New York
Brooklyn Ferry, Fulton Street
Church of the Ascension, Canal St.
City Hotel
Clinton Hall
Council Chamber, City Hall
Custom House, Wall Street
Exchange Pl., looking to Hanover Street
Grace and Trinity Churches
Junction of B'way and the Battery
Landing place foot of Barclay St.
Landing place foot of Courtlandt St.
Mansion House (Bunker's), B'way
Masonic Hall, Broadway
Merchants' Exchange, Wall St.

New York from Weehawk
Park Place, New York
Park Theater and part of Park Row
Phenix Bank, Wall Street
Public Room, Merchants' Exchange
St. George's Church, Beekman St.
St. Luke's Church, Hudson St.
St. Paul's Church, Broadway
St Patrick's Cathedral, Mott St.
St. Peter's Church, Barclay St.
St. Thomas' Church, Broadway
Steamboat Wharf, Battery Place
Steamboat Wharf, Whitehall St.
The Reservoir, Bowery
Unitarian Church, Mercer St.
U. S. Branch Bank, Wall St.
Washington Hotel, Broadway

Two plates not published in the set are

Franklin Market, Old Slip   Broadway and Fulton Street

NOTE III

" Peabody's Views," quarto. Size of the prints (two on a page), $5\frac{3}{4} \times 3\frac{3}{4}$, all except the following, which are about two inches square and are three to five on a page, viz.: The Exchange, Masonic Hall, Rotunda, U. S. Branch Bank, St. George's, Grace, St. Thomas's and Second Unitarian Churches, St. Patrick's Cathedral, Washington Hotel and Bowery Theater.

Bowery Theater, New York
Bowling Green
Broad Street, Custom House in distance
Broadway from the Park
Coffee House Slip, foot of Wall St.
City Hall
City Hotel, Grace and Trinity Churches
Deaf and Dumb Asylum
Elysian Fields, Hoboken
Grace Church, Broadway
Holt's New Hotel, corner Fulton and Water Streets
Hudson River from Hoboken
Leroy Place
Lunatic Asylum, Manhattanville
Masonic Hall, Broadway
Merchants' Exchange, Wall St.
Merchants' Room, Exchange, Wall Street

Navy Yard
New York
Park Theater, Park Row, Tammany Hall in the distance
Pearl Street and Ohio Hotel, Hanover Square in the distance
Presbyterian Church, Carmine St.
Residence of Philip Hone, Esq.
Rotunda, Chambers Street
St. George's Church, Beekman Street
St. Patrick's Cathedral, Mott St.
St. Thomas's Church, Broadway
Second Unitarian Church, Mercer corner of Prince Street
Shot Tower, East River
U. S. Branch Bank, Wall Street
Washington Institute and City Reservoir
Webb's Congress Hall, 142 B'way

NOTE IV

Blunt's "Stranger's Guide," 12mo. Size of prints about 3¾ x 2¾.

Alms House

City Hall

Coffee House Slip

South Street near Dover Street

State Prison

United States Branch Bank

NOTE V

Goodrich's "Picture of New York," 12mo. Size of prints about 3¾ x 2¾.

*Coffee House Slip

Exchange

Fulton Market

Park Theater

*South Street near Dover Street

*United States Branch Bank

View of Broadway near Grace Church

NOTE VI

Nichol's "New York Illustrated," 8vo. Size of plates 3⅜ x 2 7/10 inch, except the vignette on title and the plates, of which measurement is given.

Bellevue Hospital

Bowling Green Fountain

City Hall, 5½ x 3⅜

Custom House, present Sub-Treas'y

Deaf and Dumb Asylum

Dutch Church, Murray Street

Hall of Records

Merchants' Exchange, 5⅜ x 3⅜

New York from Governor's Island (vignette)

Post Office (old Middle Dutch Church)

Scotch Presbyterian Church, corner Grand and Crosby Streets

St. Paul's and the Astor House (5⅜ x 3 5/16)

Trinity Church, upright view, 5½ x 3½

* NOTE. Same plate as in Blunt's "Stranger's Guide."

45

NOTE VII

Plates in " New York, Past, Present and Future," added to those taken from " New York Illustrated " (Trinity and the Dutch Church in Murray street are omitted).

American Museum	Distributing Reservoir, 42nd St.
Aqueduct Bridge	Park Fountain
Baptist Church, corner Broome and Elizabeth Streets	Receiving Reservoir
	Universalist Church, Mercer St.

NOTE VIII

"ST. JOHN'S PARK" (AS IT WAS)

" St. John's Park," a highly ornamented enclosure of about four acres, situated in front of St. John's Church, and bounded by Hudson, Laight, Varick and Beach streets. It stands in the name of the Corporation of Trinity Church, though it is virtually the property of the surrounding owners and its privileges are confined to the proprietors and such others as are permitted on their recommendation to hire keys at the annual charge of ten dollars. It is surrounded by an iron fence, contains a most beautiful fountain, and is more abundantly supplied with shrubs and flowers than any other park in the city.—From " New York, Past, Present and Future."

THE GOVERNMENT HOUSE

The Government House was erected in 1790 on the site of Fort George, at the foot of Broadway, facing the Bowling Green. It was originally designed for the residence of General Washington (then President of the United States), but never occupied by him. It afterwards became the residence of Governors George Clinton and John Jay. It was used for the Custom House from the year 1799 until 1815, when it was taken down.